WELCOME!

We're glad you're here. You'll have so much fun learning German words - with cute illustrations to make them easier to remember. A few things to help you get the most out of the book:

- **100 million potential new friends:** German is spoken by over 100 million people worldwide (!) - not only in Germany, but many other countries too. Learning languages can be a powerful way to talk to more people and learn new things.

- **Double-ups:** You might notice a few words in more than one section. This is intentional, so you can easily flip to a specific section and still find the most important words. For example: "Chair" is in both the 'House' and 'Bedroom' sections.

- **Pronunciation:** You'll see a pronunciation guide under each word. This is to help you get the hang of pronouncing words in German. Example:

Der Löwe The word in German (how it's *written*).
Dehr luh-vuh Pronunciation (how it *sounds*). Sound it out to practice!
Lion English translation

With that, let's dive in. We hope you enjoy the book!

Claim Your Free Bonus Coloring Book

There's a free bonus coloring book PDF waiting for you, as a thank you for picking up this book. We think you'll like it.

Just scan the QR code below or visit
ColorCraftBooks.com/colorcraft-bonus.

Kids: Make sure to ask a parent!

Scan to get your free
coloring
book download

Table of Contents

LANDTIERE

LAND ANIMALS

Der Löwe

Dehr luh-vuh

Lion

Der Elefant

Dehr eh-leh-fahnt

Elephant

Der Tiger

Dehr tee-guh

Tiger

Die Giraffe

Dee gee-rah-fuh

Giraffe

Der Bär

Dehr bear

Bear

1

Das Zebra
Dahs tsay-bruh

Zebra

Der Wolf
Dehr vawlf

Wolf

Das Nashorn
Dahs nahs-horn

Rhinoceros

Der Leopard
Dehr leh-oh-pahr

Leopard

Der Gepard
Dehr geh-pahr

Cheetah

Das Känguru

Dahs kehn-goo-roo

Kangaroo

Das Flusspferd

Dahs floos-faird

Hippopotamus

Der Gorilla

Dehr goh-ree-lah

Gorilla

Der Büffel

Dehr boo-fel

Buffalo

Der Fuchs

Dehr fooks

Fox

Der Hirsch

Dehr hirsh

Deer

Das Kamel

Dahs kah-mehl

Camel

Der Panda

Dehr pahn-dah

Panda

Das Koala

Dahs koh-ah-lah

Koala

Die Hyäne

Dee hee-eh-nuh

Hyena

HAUSTIERE

PETS

Der Hund

Dehr hoond

Dog

Der Vogel

Dehr voh-guhl

Bird

Die Katze

Dee kah-tze

Cat

Der Fisch

Dehr fish

Fish

Das Meerschweinchen

Dahs meer-shvine-chen

Hamster

Der Hase
Dehr hah-zeh
Rabbit

Das Schwein
Dahs shvayn
Guinea Pig

Die Schildkröte
Dee shild-kro-teh
Turtle

Der Papagei
Dehr pah-pah-guy
Parrot

Die Schlange
Dee shlahn-guh
Snake

NUTZTIERE

FARM ANIMALS

Die Kuh
Dee koo
Cow

Das Huhn
Dahs hoon
Chicken

Das Schwein
Dahs shvayn
Pig

Das Pferd
Dahs faird
Horse

Das Schaf
Dahs shaf
Sheep

Die Ziege
Dee tsay-guh

Goat

Die Pute
Dee poo-tuh

Turkey

Die Ente
Dee en-tuh

Duck

Der Hahn
Dehr hahn

Rooster

Der Esel
Dehr ay-zel

Donkey

MEERESLEBE

WESEN

SEA ANIMALS

Der Fisch
Dehr fish
Fish

Der Wal
Dehr vahl
Whale

Der Delfin
Dehr del-feen
Dolphin

Der Hai
Dehr high
Shark

Der Oktopus
DER OK-toh-poos
Octopus

Der Seestern
Dehr zay-stern

Starfish

Die Qualle
Dee kwah-leh

Jellyfish

Die Meeresschildkröte
Dee mare-eh-shild-kroh-tuh

Sea Turtle

Das Seepferdchen
Dahs zay-pair-dchen

Seahorse

Der Kalmar
Dehr kal-mar

Squid

VÖGEL

BIRDS

Der Uhu
Dehr oo-hoo

Owl

Der Falke
Dehr fahl-kuh

Falcon

Der Adler
Dehr ah-dler

Eagle

Der Specht
Dehr shpacht

Woodpecker

Der Spatz
Dehr shpats

Sparrow

Der Rabe

Dehr rah-beh

Crow

Das Rebhuhn

Dahs reb-huhn

Partridge

Die Taube

Dee tau-beh

Pigeon

Das Rotkehlchen

Dahs roht-kayl-khen

Robin

Der Falke

Dehr fahl-kuh

Falcon

WALDTIERE

FOREST ANIMALS

Der Hirsch
Dehr hirsh

Deer

Das Eichhörnchen
Dahs eye-khoorn-chin

Squirrel

Der Bär
Dehr bear

Bear

Der Fuchs
Dehr fooks

Fox

Der Waschbär
Dehr vash-bear

Raccoon

18

Das Stinktier
das SHTINK-teer
Skunk

Der Biber
der BEE-ber
Beaver

Das Wildschwein
Dahs vild-shvayn
Wild Boar

Der Igel
der EE-gel
Hedgehog

Der Elch
der ELCH
Moose

INSEKTEN

INSECTS

Der Schmetterling

der SHMET-er-ling

Butterfly

Die Ameise

dee AH-my-zeh

Ant

Der Marienkäfer

der MAH-ree-en-
kay-fer

Ladybug

Die Heuschrecke

dee HOY-shreh-keh

Grasshopper

Die Libelle

dee lee-BELL-eh

Dragonfly

21

Die Raupe

dee ROW-peh

Caterpillar

Das Glühwürmchen

dahs GLUE-voorm-chen

Firefly

Die Biene

dee BEE-neh

Bee

Die Motte

dee MOTT-eh

Moth

Die Grille

dee GREE-leh

Cricket

DIE SCHULE

SCHOOL

Das Klassenzimmer

das KLAH-sen-tsee-
mer

Classroom

Der Schüler

der SHU-luh-er

Student

Der Lehrer

der LEHR-er

Teacher

Der Schreibtisch

der SHRYB-tish

Desk

Der Stuhl

der SHTOOL

Chair

Der Stift

der SHTIFT

Pen

Der Bleistift

der BLY-sh-tift

Pencil

Das Notizbuch

das noh-TEETS-book

Notebook

Die Tafel

dee TAH-fel

Chalkboard

Die Kreide

dee KRY-deh

Chalk

Das Buch

das BOOK

Book

Das Lineal

das LI-nee-ahl

Ruler

Der Radiergummi

der rah-DEER-gum-ee

Eraser

Der Rucksack

der RUCK-sack

Backpack

Der Marker

der MAHR-ker

Marker

Der Schulbus
der SHOOL-bus

School Bus

Der Klebestift
der KLEH-beh-shtift

Glue Stick

Der Wachsmalstift
der VAHKS-mahl-shtift

Crayon

Die Schere
dee SHAY-reh

Scissors

Der Taschenrechner
der TAH-shen-raych-ner

Calculator

SPORT

SPORTS

Der Fußball
der FOOZ-bahl
Soccer/Football

Der Basketball
der BAH-sket-bahl
Basketball

Der Baseball
der BASE-bahl
Baseball

Das Tennis
das TEN-nis
Tennis

Das Schwimmen
das SHVIM-men
Swimming

29

Die Gymnastik
dee GUYM-nah-stik

Gymnastics

Das Hockey
das HAWK-ay

Hockey

Der Volleyball
der VOL-ley-bahl

Volleyball

Das Laufen
das LOW-fen

Running

Das Rugby
das RUG-bee

Rugby

FARBEN

COLORS

Rot

ROHT

Red

Grün

GROON

Green

Blau

BLOW

Blue

Gelb

GELB

Yellow

Orange

oh-RAHN-jeh

Orange

Rosa

ROH-sah

Pink

Schwarz

SHVAHR-ts

Black

Lila

LEE-lah

Purple

Weiß

VYCE

White

Grau

GROU

Gray

Braun

BROWN

Brown

Silber

ZILL-ber

Silver

Gold

GOLD

Gold

Hellblau

HEL-blow

Light Blue

34

Dunkelgrün

DOON-kel-groon

Dark Green

Hellrosa

HEL-roh-sah

Light Pink

Cyanblau

SYAN-blou

Cyan

Beige

BEY-zhe

Beige

Violett

VEE-oh-lett

Violet

Türkis

TER-kis

Turquoise

BASTELN

CRAFTS

Das Papier

das PAH-peer

Paper

Die Schere

dee SHAY-reh

Scissors

Der Kleber

der KLEH-ber

Glue

Der Klebestreifen

der KLEH-beh-sht-
ray-fen

Sticky Tape

Die Aufkleber

dee OWF-kleh-ber

Stickers

Die Filzstifte
dee FILTZ-shtift-eh

Markers

Die Buntstifte
dee BOONT-shtift-eh

Colored Pencils

Die Wachsmalstifte
dee VAHKS-mahl-shtift-eh

Crayons

Die Farbe
dee FAHR-beh

Paint

Der Pinsel
der PIN-sel

Paintbrush

FAMILIE

FAMILY

Die Mutter

dee MOOT-er

Mother

Der Vater

der FAH-ter

Father

Der Bruder

der BROO-der

Brother

Die Schwester

dee SHVES-ter

Sister

Die Tante

dee TAHN-teh

Aunt

Der Onkel

der OHN-kel

Uncle

Die Cousine

dee koo-ZEE-neh

Cousin (female)

Der Cousin

der KOO-zeng

Cousin (male)

Die Oma

dee OH-mah

Grandma

Der Opa

der OH-pah

Grandpa

Der Sohn

der ZOHN

Son

Der Neffe

der NEH-feh

Nephew

Die Tochter

dee TOCH-ter

Daughter

Die Nichte

dee NEECH-teh

Niece

Das Baby

das BAY-bee

Baby

Der Enkel
der EN-kel
Grandson

Die Enkelin
dee EN-kel-in
Granddaughter

Die Eltern
dee EL-tern
Parents

Die Kinder
dee KIN-der
Children

Die Verwandten
dee fer-VANT-en
Relatives

DAS HAUS

THE HOUSE

Das Schlafzimmer

das SHLAF-tsi-mer

Bedroom

Die Küche

dee KOO-cheh

Kitchen

Das Wohnzimmer

das VON-tsim-mer

Living Room

Das Badezimmer

das BAH-deh-tsee-mer

Bathroom

Der Flur

der FLOOR

Hallway

Das Fenster

das FEN-ster

Window

Das Dach

das DAHK

Roof

Die Tür

dee TEWR

Door

Der Hof

der HAWF

Yard

Der Teppich

der TEP-pish

Carpet

Die Treppe
dee TREH-peh

Stairs

Die Wand
dee VANT

Wall

Der Boden
der BOH-den

Floor

Die Decke
dee DEK-eh

Ceiling

Der Stuhl
der SHTOOL

Chair

Der Tisch

der TISH

Table

Die Lampe

dee LAHM-peh

Lamp

Das Sofa

das SOH-fah

Couch

Der Schrank

der SHRAHNK

Closet

Das Waschbecken

das VAHSH-beck-en

Sink

DIE KÜCHE

THE KITCHEN

Das Waschbecken
das VAHSH-beck-en

Sink

Der Kochtopf
der KOCH-topf

Pot

Die Pfanne
dee FAN-neh

Pan

Die Tasse
dee TAH-sseh

Cup

Der Teller
der TEL-er

Plate

Die Gabel
dee GAH-bel

Fork

Das Messer
das MEH-ser

Knife

Der Löffel
der LER-fel

Spoon

Der Herd
der HAIRD

Stove

Der Ofen
der OH-fen

Oven

DAS SCHLAFZIMMER

THE BEDROOM

Das Bett
das BETT
Bed

Das Kissen
das KIS-sen
Pillow

Die Decke
dee DEK-eh
Blanket

Das Nachtlicht
das NAHCHT-licht
Nightlight

Die Spielzeuge
dee SHPEEL-tsoy-geh
Toys

Die Kommode

dee ko-MOH-deh

Dresser

Der Teppich

der TEP-pich

Rug

Die Lampe

dee LAHM-peh

Lamp

Der Schrank

der SHRAHNK

Closet

Das Bücherregal

das BYOO-chuh-ray-gahl

Bookshelf

DER KÖRPER

THE BODY

Der Kopf
der KOPF

Head

Das Gesicht
das geh-ZICH-t

Face

Die Augen
dee OW-gin

Eyes

Die Ohren
dee OH-ren

Ears

Die Nase
dee NAH-zeh

Nose

Der Mund

der MOONT

Mouth

Die Zähne

dee TSEH-neh

Teeth

Die Haare

dee HA-reh

Hair

Der Hals

der HALS

Neck

Die Schultern

dee SHUL-tern

Shoulders

Die Arme

dee AHR-meh

Arms

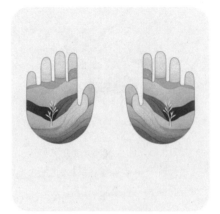

Die Hände

dee HEN-deh

Hands

Die Finger

dee FING-er

Fingers

Die Beine

dee BYE-neh

Legs

Die Füße

dee FUE-seh

Feet

Die Zehen
dee TSEH-en

Toes

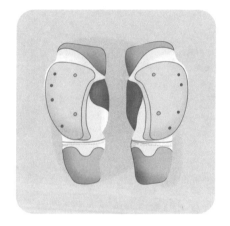

Die Knie
dee KNEE-eh

Knees

Die Ellbogen
dee EL-bo-gen

Elbows

Der Rücken
der ROO-ken

Back

Die Brust
dee BROOST

Chest

DER PARK

THE PARK

Der Baum

der BOWM

Tree

Der Spielplatz

der SHPEEL-platz

Playground

Die Schaukel

dee SHOW-kel

Swing

Die Rutsche

dee ROO-tcheh

Slide

Die Bank

dee BANK

Bench

61

Das Gras
das GRAHS

Grass

Der Brunnen
der BROON-en

Fountain

Der Weg
der VAYG

Path

Der Picknicktisch
der PICK-nik-tish

Picnic Table

Die Blume
dee BLOO-meh

Flower

DER STRAND

THE BEACH

Der Sand
der ZAND
Sand

Der Ozean
der OH-zeh-ahn
Ocean

Die Wellen
dee VELL-en
Waves

Die Muschel
dee MOO-shel
Seashell

Das Strandtuch
das SHTRAND-tooh
Beach Towel

64

Der Sonnenschirm

der ZON-nen-sherm

Umbrella

Die Sonnencreme

dee ZON-en-krehm

Sunblock

Der Rettungsschwimmer

der REH-toong-shvim-mer

Lifeguard

Der Strandball

der SHTRAND-ball

Beach Ball

Die Sonnenbrille

dee ZON-en-bril-leh

Sunglasses

DER

BAUERNHOF

THE FARM

Der Traktor

der TRAK-tor

Tractor

Das Heu

das HOY

Hay

Die Scheune

dee SHOY-neh

Barn

Der Zaun

der TSAUN

Fence

Das Feld

das FELD

Field

Das Silo
das SEE-loh

Silo

Der Pflug
der FLOOG

Plow

Der Bauer
der BOW-er

Farmer

Die Schubkarre
dee SHOOB-kar-reh

Wheelbarrow

Die Vogelscheuche
dee VOH-gel-shoy-cheh

Scarecrow

Claim Your Free Bonus Coloring Book

There's a free bonus coloring book PDF waiting for you, as a thank you for picking up this book. We think you'll like it.

Just scan the QR code below or visit
ColorCraftBooks.com/colorcraft-bonus.

Kids: Make sure to ask a parent!

Scan to get your free
coloring
book download

Danke!

Thanks so much for picking up this book. We hope you enjoyed
reading it as much
as we enjoyed making it!

If you liked it, we'd love if you could leave a review. This helps
other people discover the book.

We're always releasing more books for active kids, so if you'd like to
find other exciting books like this one, please come visit us at the
links below.

Thanks again,
The team at Color Craft Books

ColorCraftBooks.com
@ColorCraftBooks

Made in United States
Troutdale, OR
11/24/2024

25277627R00042